A BEGINNER'S GUIDE TO DEVELOPING YOUR INTUITION

MARION MCGEOUGH

© Marion McGeough all rights reserved

All rights reserved. This book may not be reproduced, transmitted, or stored in whole or in part by any means including graphic, electronic or mechanical without expressed written consent of the publisher/author except in the case of brief quotations embodied in critical articles and reviews. The right of Marion McGeough to be identified as the author/owner of this work has been asserted by them in accordance with the Copyright, Designs and Patents Act 1988.

Published by Marion McGeough.

All rights reserved. No part of this publication may be reproduced, stored in a retrieval system or transmitted in any form or by any means, electronic, mechanical, photocopying, recording or otherwise without the prior permission of the publisher.

While the publisher has taken reasonable care in the preparation of this book, the publisher makes no representation, express or implied, with regard to the accuracy of the information contained in this book and cannot accept legal responsibility or liability for any errors or omissions from the book or the consequences thereof.

Products or services that are referred to in this book may be either trademarks and/or registered trademarks of their respective owners. The publisher and author make no claims to these trademarks.

A CIP Catalogue record for this book is available from the British Library.

Formatting and cover design by ebook-designs.co.uk

This is a work of fiction. The events and characters described herein are imaginary and are not intended to refer to specific places or living persons. The opinions expressed in this manuscript are solely the opinions of the author.

INTRODUCTION

Welcome

Welcome to a world of discovery and of self-discovery. As a psychotherapist, hypnotherapist, Reiki healer and intuitive, I hold a certain fascination for people and their behaviour. Why are some people happy and others sad? Why do some seem to sail through life with little difficulty, when others seem to experience tragedy, poverty and ill health throughout their lives? Some of you may be thinking that most of us are born to suffer, with only a lucky few, the elite, who have an abundance of health, wealth and happiness. Well let me tell you that this is not the way life is supposed to be. We were all born to have a happy and fulfilled life, it is just that we may stray too far from the path that is right for us and find that everything goes terribly wrong.

A few years ago, I remember looking at a woman as she stepped from her chauffeur driven car onto the pavement, and thinking I would give anything to be her right now. How silly I was. I imagined that she lived in a beautiful house and that she took exotic holidays. I thought that she would not have to worry about paying the bills and she could go into any store and buy anything and everything she chose. I remember feeling envious, inferior and helpless.

Looking back and analysing my feelings, it was not that I wanted to be this other woman, this stranger, who had briefly crossed my path. No, I wanted the freedom she had and I wanted to feel good about myself and my purpose in life. When a person believes that they have very little in the way of financial freedom or good health or anything else that is lacking in their lives, it is not that they wish to be someone else, it is that they want to be free from what is causing them anguish, pain and sorrow. Unfortunately, some people will do anything to remove the pain from within. If only they knew that if they listened to what their body and mind was trying to tell them, then the emotional pain and any associated feelings would go away. It is often when people are at breaking point, when they can no longer handle the inner turmoil that they seek therapy and that is when people like me enter their lives.

These days I see clients for therapy from many different types of backgrounds. I often see stressed out business executives who wish that they had never climbed the corporate ladder to "success". It is lonely at the top they often tell me. There is always someone willing to take your place, waiting for you to make that vital mistake. Those working below them often hate them and the long hours can create havoc on family life. Many take medication for indigestion. Heart or blood pressure problems are also common due to the stress. At times, I think back to that image of the business executive getting out of her car and I wonder if she was/is a truly happy person or if she is living a life fraught with anxiety.

Whenever I see clients who "look" successful and, when speaking with them during therapy, I am often reminded by the words they say and the pain they express; that our physical appearance is for the outside world only. A client may look the part of a confident and competent professional, often speaking in an authoritarian way, commanding action and attention with each sentence. Inside they may feel like a child, perhaps waiting to be "caught out" and told that they are not good enough for the job. They feel that there is something missing, that they can't quite put their finger on it but it seems as if something is not quite right. There is a huge difference between their interior and exterior worlds.

For those people who have never actually had therapy themselves they may be under the misconception that those who do seek therapy are from odd, strange, tragic or difficult circumstances. Whilst all of this is true for some, there is also a belief that there must be something deeply wrong with an individual if they are unable to sort out their heads themselves and that they need to seek therapy in order to function "normally". This is far from the truth. A person often seeks therapy because they can no longer stand the pain and anguish that they are currently experiencing.

When I first began seeing clients I used to find it fascinating to meet people who I assumed had it all. Coming from a poor background myself I always thought that financial success was all that was needed for happiness. I was fascinated to discover that the rich had the same problems as the poor! Clients would mention that when they were children they had it all: A "good" upbringing with both parents happy together. There was financial stability with either one of both parents working good jobs or having their own business. As a child they were healthy and did well at school and even university. Then at some stage, something went wrong. Perhaps the family dynamics and circumstances had changed. The parents may have become a little older and have altered their views on bringing up children, there may be more or less money readily available to buy gifts and treats, or they may live in a worse/better area. What is often forgotten about is that we all have our own life path, our purpose which we need to follow. It is when we listen to our intuitive side that we connect with our life purpose and we become whole again.

The secret, to a satisfying and fulfilling life is to use the power within. The mind is a magical, fascinating part of us. Most of us pay attention to the way we look, some of us spending a small fortune on grooming products, clothes and gym memberships. If we find something physically wrong with us we go to the doctor and sort it out. Often we may be vigilant and seek medical attention if we notice a spot is growing or we feel frequently tired. We even look after our pets better than we do ourselves. What we are not good at is looking after our minds and listening to the messages that our body is trying to tell us.

This book will show you how easy it is for you to pay attention to those messages. If you fail to pay attention to what is going on in your mind you will suffer the consequences sooner or later. It is equally as important to learn to pay attention and develop your intuition. You must learn how to develop your intuition so that you can become heathier and happier, whole again.

During my therapy sessions the techniques I use often focus on the conscious mind. Typically, a client attends for between several weeks to several months depending on the type of issues raised both before and during therapy and the complexity of those issues. When a client talks during the session they are speaking with words from both the conscious and the pre-conscious mind. The pre-conscious acts as a sort of gatekeeper between the conscious and the unconscious. If there is a good relationship between the client and the therapist the client is able to relax more and when asked to recall information whilst awake, the client is able to do so in greater details due to the relaxed state that they are in.

One of the keys to successful therapy is goal setting. A person needs to know what they want and how they are going to get there. As you learn to develop your intuition you must also bear a goal or question in mind. During therapy the goal may change a little and therefore it is redefined, but overall goal setting makes sense; after all, you would not go on a walk and not know where you are going would you?

So, during therapy the goal is set and the client is happy and comfortable with the relationship with the therapist. All seems to be going well for the first few sessions. The client begins to see the nature of the problem and begins to understand the cause of it. Great. The next step is to change the thoughts connected to the perceived problem and any behaviour associated with it. This is where the difficulty lies. Mentally, the person knows that their fear of spiders, dogs, buttons, clowns, driving, water, spoons, shoe laces and many, many others, as well as a fear of being too thin, too fat, too old, or too short are not based on the present but on some past experience. Even a person with PTSD knows at a rational level that the sound of fireworks are not gunfire but those of fireworks. What is often difficult is finding a way of getting the person to truly accept the difference between the past and the present.

Our conscious mind makes connections in order to make sense of the world. If we see a person walking down the road in the distance wearing a green coat and one of our friends has a green coat we may initially be mistaken that this person is our friend. Our conscious mind looks for similar patterns in order to make connections. Many people know this but what most do not know is that our intuition plays an important role. We are directed in nearly all that we do by our intuition. As you read this book you too will lean the importance and value of developing your intuition.

Hypnotherapy is another tool that I use to "speak" to the subconscious mind directly. Typically, the client goes into a trance and the deeper the better. The depth of the trance is due to the skill of the therapist as well as the willingness of the client. During the first session the client may only go into a light trance. This is because the conscious mind is "thinking", hey I need to keep awake to see what is going on here.

During the session the client will reveal information which is not readily available during "normal" therapy. This is often information which is painful or traumatic and has been blocked by the conscious and pre-conscious mind as a way of protecting the person from pain. The problem occurs when a person is unable to lead a "normal" life due to the repressed emotions.

Hypnotherapy is also used in order to help a person make changes in their lives. It is not unusual for a person to seek hypnotherapy for weight loss and to stop smoking for example. What is less well known is that a skilled hypnotherapist can be seen to assist a client by treating eczema, stopping nose bleeds and even be present during surgery when a client cannot or does not want anaesthetic. Hypnotherapy works because it utilises the most powerful part of you, your subconscious mind and the power of your intuition.

When we engage the subconscious mind our intuition is also engaged as all of our thoughts and feelings are expressed. This is the true magic of the mind. Now, this book is not about hypnotherapy or any other type of therapy. This book is about allowing YOU to connect with the magical part of the mind and allowing you to begin to develop your intuition. Your subconscious mind and your intuition work together. As you connect deeply within your own mind, life will become easier. You will be walking down your own life path, not one which has been created for you by someone else, no matter how well intended. Imagine achieving the answers to your problems, wishes and desires all to be found within yourself. If you still doubt what I say, or if you still do not believe that your mind is all powerful, then I would like you to try this exercise out. Please read the information below in full before trying out the exercise.

- Sit somewhere quiet where you will not be disturbed.

- Play some relaxing music if you think it will help you to relax.

- Sit this way for several minutes until you begin to feel very, very relaxed almost like you are going to sleep.

- Now, I want you to imagine that you are feeling very, very cold. Imagine that you are outside in a blizzard and feel the cold on your skin. If this is difficult for you or perhaps you live in a warm climate and have never experienced a cold climate imagine that you have just put your hand and arm into a freezer and feel the cold, numbing sensation in one of your arms.

- When you have felt cold for a couple of minutes bring your focus back into the room and you will feel your temperature return to normal.

How did this work for you?

For some it may work better than others. You could also reverse the exercise by imaging that you are steadily getting warmer and warmer. Perhaps you are sitting out in the sun or perhaps you are sitting next to an open fire. If you are still sceptical think back to a time when you watched a really sad or happy film. Remember those feelings that you had? I bet you laughed and even cried (or at least felt sad) at the appropriate times.

This book is about YOU living the life that you want to and about YOU being able to access the magic of your intuition, the power within. You will be shown how to do this so that you will be healthier and happier than you ever thought possible. All you have to do is follow the exercises and practice. Your focus will be taken internally not externally so that you can listen to what your intuition and inner voice is telling you. Begin to learn to listen to the messages from within; I am certain that you will be glad that you did.

THE BRAIN

Experience each moment to its fullest.
A Zen Proverb

The brain is a fascinating organ. It is the centre of the nervous system and it is wonderfully complex. Did you know, for example, that the cerebral cortex contains 15 to 33 billion neurons? Each neuron is connected by synapses to thousands of other neurons. A synapse allows a neuron to pass an electrical or chemical signal from one cell to another. This is important not only for the body to function but for the transportation of other signals, more on this later. Neurons communicate by protoplasmic fibres called axons. These carry signal pulses throughout the body and the brain.

The brain stem is situated at the posterior part of the brain which is continuous with the spinal cord. The brain stem consists of the medulla oblongata, pons and the midbrain. All information from the cerebrum and cerebellum pass through the brain stem. Imagine thousands and thousands of signals sending messages passing back and forth and most of the time we are not even aware of it happening. The brain stem also regulates our responses to pain, our body temperature and even our sensations of pressure. The brain is responsible for cardiovascular control, respiratory control, levels of alertness and awareness and our consciousness. Wow, with all of these functions is it any wonder that a scientist can spend a whole lifetime studying and researching the brain and still not truly understand its true potential.

As well as the brain, each of us has a mind. It is very, very important to learn how to use your mind properly. Unfortunately, most of have not been taught how to use the mind. This is not the result of neglect by our parents and caregivers. No. This is simply because they also did not know how to use the mind either. Whilst the brain contains physical matter; cells, blood vessels and so on, the mind contains thoughts and it is those thoughts that lead to feelings and emotions. The brain has a physical place in the body; the mind does not and is therefore limitless. As it is limitless imagine the boundless opportunities that the mind can present.

Most people are aware of the conscious mind and the unconscious mind. The conscious mind is the part of the mind that we are aware of and is responsible for our thoughts and most of our movements. For example, if we are thinking about going on holiday our conscious mind will rationally think about how long the holiday will be, how much we can afford to spend and where we would like to go.

It may seem as if our conscious thoughts are the boss, they decide what we are going to do, say and think. Wrong. The conscious mind simply accepts all that is presented before it.

Which of the following 2 paragraphs would generally identify what you were told as a child?

1. You are a clever boy/girl. You can do anything you choose to do. You are so witty. You are a handsome boy/beautiful girl. We all love you. The world is a safe and wonderful place. People are generally kind and honest. Work hard and you will be rewarded. Be kind and polite to others. Set goals and achieve them.

OR

2. You are so stupid. You never do anything right. Our sort never gets on in life. Don't trust anyone; they are all out to get you. Do the minimum you can in your job. Don't bother to think about college, it's a waste of time/money. You will end up in a dead end job just like me. You are just plain and average. You have ideas above your "station" in life.

Naturally the child who is nurtured and encouraged and shown love in early life will begin to believe it. If a child is told that he will never amount to anything there is a greater chance that he will begin to believe and just accept it and this belief will lead to a self- fulfilling prophecy. You need to be smart. You must begin to choose to listen to your inner voice as your intuition will tell you the answers to your questions. Even if you have come from the most poor and humble background imaginable you still have dreams and aspirations. No one can take your dreams and ambitions away from you unless you allow them to. There is nothing in the outer world that has not existed in someone's inner world. You simply have to learn how to use what you have inside of you and this book will show you how.

A close friend has two sons. When asked to describe them as children my friend said that they were very different. Tom was always ready to please others, he was kind thoughtful and went out of his way to help other people. In order to please his parents he went onto medical school and eventually became a doctor. To the outside world he seems to have it all. He is married to a psychiatrist and they have a small child. When speaking with him he stated that he feels as if something is missing in his life. He had always wanted to be an architect like his brother, Sam but he had wanted to please his parents and he was good at science. He said that he felt that he was just an average doctor and that he felt in his heart that he would have been an excellent architect as this was what he truly wanted to be.

Sam had been an entirely different child to Tom. Sam had always challenged and asked questions as to why he had to do things. He had challenged his teachers, caregivers and parents, sometimes driving them a little crazy! Sam was very good in subjects that he liked and enjoyed and difficult in subjects that he disliked. Sam had been excellent at art and he was now a CEO in a major architectural company with offices all around the world. Sam is also married and his wife is a stay at home mom to their two small girls. Sam said that although he believed that his behaviour in his youth had been a little problematic at times he believes that his success in life is due to his ability to listen to his inner voice and that many of his decisions in life have come not only from factual information presented to him but from an inner voice, a gut instinct guiding him.

When meeting with both men I could see that both were not unhappy, however Sam had an inner glow a sense of vitality which far outshone that of his brother. This, I believe, stems from living your life to your true potential and living it not for other people, but for yourself. So, now it is time for you to begin to shine.

DEVELOPING AWARENESS

**How are you feeling at the moment?
What are you thinking?**
What you think is what you ultimately feel. Your thoughts become things. What you think can manifest into something wonderful or something awful; you have the power to decide which. Whilst all of this does indeed sound great, what you have to realise, from this moment forward, is that YOU have control of your thoughts and actions. With control comes responsibility. By learning how to slow ourselves down and listen to our intuition we are able to change our lives. Remember that life is a gift not to be wasted. You have the responsibility and the power to live a productive and healthy life of your choosing.

Begin to Develop Your Intuition
Begin to tap in to your intuition by carrying out this simple exercise:

Find a quiet space where you will not be disturbed. You may choose to sit on a chair. If you do this ensure that you have adequate back support. If you are sitting on the floor ensure that you really are comfortable. Do not cross your legs if this makes you feel uncomfortable. Try not to lie on a bed as you may fall asleep! Ensure that you are sitting up straight but not ramrod straight as this may cause some discomfort as well.

Choose a time of day that is peaceful and you will not have to rush off and do something else after carrying out this session.

- Begin by controlling your breathing. To do this begin by counting as you take a deep breath in through your nose for a count of 6 and out through your mouth for a count of 6.

- Keep breathing in this way for around 3 minutes.

- The purpose of the breathing aspect of this exercise is for you to focus inwardly. When doing this you are paying less attention to the outside world and closing down the outside stimuli. As you do this you become still in both your body and mind as you begin to focus internally.

- Now that you have been breathing slowly and deeply I want you to become aware of any fleeting thoughts you may have.

- The tricky bit, at least at the beginning, is to just become aware of those thoughts. Do not dwell on them. See the thoughts as passing clouds and allow them to drift.

- After several more minutes bring your conscious awareness back into the room and focus once more on your environment.

What were your thoughts?

Did you surprise yourself?

This exercise is often difficult the first time it is carried out. In a hectic world it is often hard to really let go. Some people come up with lists in their head of things they "have" or want to do. Some find it difficult to let go of fleeting thoughts. If you have found it difficult then that is okay. With practice it will become easier as you develop your intuition and your awareness of both your body and your mind increases.

Now back to the exercise, here is what 3 people discovered when carrying it out for the first time:

Angela aged 22: I thought of my new job and I was not sure if I really liked it. That surprised me because I had told everyone that it was okay. The pay is good for someone of my age and there are prospects. It's just that I am not sure that the other girls like me and this is what makes me feel uncomfortable. I then had to really push the idea from my mind as I had wanted a chance to see what other thoughts would come into my mind. I began to think about my sister, who is pregnant and that soon I would be an auntie. Then I began to think about lists of things that I had to do and I realised that my time was up as I was just getting restless and I had lost my focus.

Brian aged 42: I found it hard to focus on my breathing to start with. I am usually such an active person and I found that sitting down and just focusing on my breathing was a waste of time to begin with. Then I began to feel waves of sadness sweep over me. My brother's wife, Amy had died a couple of months ago. She had been a lovely lady and I knew that my brother had been finding it difficult to cope. I felt sadness and guilt as I had not been spending much time with my brother. I then decided that I wanted to call him so I ended the exercise. I have now made arrangements to spend a long weekend at his house. He lives on the other side of the country and I am looking forward to seeing him in the next couple of weeks. I feel better inside as my gut told me that this was the right thing to do.

Susan aged 58: I found this exercise really easy because I meditate twice a week and I do Yoga almost daily. To begin with I felt really relaxed, as I had expected. I did not think that I would discover anything that I did not know about myself. Then as thoughts gently floated past my mind I began to think about retiring from my job. I am not sure where this came from. I am a medical secretary and up until that moment the thought of retirement never entered my mind. I will give this some further exploration and see where it takes me. I must admit that the idea is quite appealing!

Angela, Brian and Susan, if asked, would probably have said that they knew themselves quite well. This clearly is not the case. We only know part of ourselves. Come with me on a journey of self-discovery and learn how to tap into your true self by learning to use your intuition.

GETTING STARTED

If you can imagine it, you can achieve it.
If you can dream it, you can become it.
William Arthur Ward

When time began life was very simple. People were divided into tribes. You were part of that tribe and you had a role to play. Any outsiders were the enemy. Later groups of people became families sharing a family name to connect them. As well as saying their name, nowadays most people identify who they are by their occupations. A man may proudly say that he is a doctor. Another man may say, with less pride, that he is a labourer. Unfortunately we tend to associate a lot more value to some occupations than others. The truth is that we need both doctors and labourers. The doctor may deliver the baby but if the builder does not build suitable houses (shelter) the baby will not have anywhere to live.

Our jobs do not define who we are. Our job is merely something that we do in order to make a living. Granted, some jobs or vocations will give a more clear understanding of who a person is at a soul level than others. If one person chooses to enter the field of medicine he is more likely than not to be of a caring disposition.

To begin to develop your intuition you must be honest with yourself. Nowadays people are rushing to buy books to help them discover their true selves. They feel that something is missing in their lives. Desperate to discover what this is they buy book after book hoping that the answer will be found somewhere in the text. This is where they are wrong. The answer, my friend, lies within you. This is why being totally honest with yourself is important because only you know what is right for you. Only you can find that missing piece of the jigsaw. How do you do this I hear you ask? Well, this book is here to guide you and to help you discover the path in life that is right for you. Once shown, you may never leave it. Your intuition will be your personal guide for life.

Practical exercise

In order to establish how close or how far away you are from your true self, I want you to carry out this exercise:

Create two columns: The left column is headed TASK and the right column is headed COMMENTS.

I want you to list all of the tasks that you carry out on a typical day and in the comments column I want you to put down how you felt. See a very simple example below, it may help you before you get started:

TASK	COMMENT
Getting ready for work	Bored/ tired/ heavy.
At work	Time stood still, felt sad.
Lunch	Freedom lasting 1 hour.
Evening	Relaxed, light & free.

Now I want you to read what you have written down. Are most of the comments positive or negative? Perhaps some are neutral. How do you feel after carrying out this simple exercise? Do you feel generally content with life or do you feel as if something is missing? My guess is that you feel okay, just drifting along. Let me tell you, this is one of the worst states to be in. Why you may ask? Because when you feel this way you are not motivated to change and to develop because it is often too much effort to become who you really want to become. It is easier and safer to just put up with things instead.

I asked a friend to carry out the above exercise. This is what he wrote. (Note the different format to what I have suggested above. When carrying out this exercise, present it the best way to suit yourself.)

TASK: Getting up and ready for work.

COMMENT: Anger - hate my job - dislike my manager - feel as if I must change direction - thought of calling in sick - in a bad mood - unable to think of anything positive.

TASK: Breakfast

COMMENT: Enjoy doing this – get to spend time with my girls (aged 4 &7) - also get to read the newspaper - a little me time - time to catch up with Helen, my wife.

TASK: Work

COMMENT: Glad to see Craig back from his hols - not looking forward to the meeting and reports that will have to be completed by the pm.

TASK: Journey to and from work

COMMENT: I hate this with a passion - spend 2 hrs per day on a train – feel as if it a waste of my life - mind wanders and inner voice tells me begin to work for myself.

The purpose of the above exercise is twofold:

Firstly, it is giving you chance to have a few quiet minutes and for you to freely express your thoughts and feelings in writing. This is a therapeutic exercise on its own.

Secondly, you are connecting with your vibrational frequency and you are starting to question aspects of your life. If you had lots of negative comments your vibrational frequency will be low and if you found that you had lots of positive comments your vibrations will be much higher. The higher the vibrations the easier it is for your body to recover from illness and the less likely it is that you will become ill in the first place. I bet you know someone who is unhappy with their lot in life and they are often ill suffering from aches or pains, or perhaps they have frequent colds. This is all because they have low vibrations and are not in touch with their soul, not listening to their intuition. Are you now ready to discover more about yourself? Are you ready to move forward and begin to develop your senses?

YOUR SENSES

Observe, record, tabulate and communicate. Use your five senses to learn to hear, learn to feel, learn to smell. Learn to see and know that by practice alone you can become an expert.
Unknown

Your senses are the key to your intuition. As a child you were not encouraged to develop your senses, your education was based on facts and figures. Your intuition has always been with you and always will be with you. You use your intuition all of the time and most of the time you are totally unaware of it. Have you ever said, felt or thought:

- Uncomfortable when meeting someone for the first time and not known why.

- Had a dream that was vivid and came true.

- Had a little "inner voice" telling you not to go somewhere or do something but chose to ignore it to your detriment.

- Knew that something felt right or wrong but could not say why?

When we receive messages via our intuition we often choose to ignore them. Often we tend to laugh at ourselves. I myself have said in the past, if only I had listened to my "little voice" telling me to slow down. This was before I began to listen to my intuition and now life is so much easier.

The ways that we receive messages via our intuition are usually closely related to the way that we make sense and interpret our world. If you remember directions by remembering the words that someone tells you, you are likely to receive messages from your inner voice. If you can visualise where you are going you are likely to receive visual messages. If you simply have a feeling that you are going the right way or doing the right thing, you are likely to use your kinaesthetic sense.

One of your senses is more highly developed than the others. Begin by discovering which of your senses is the most developed.

The Visual Sense
I remember once watching a movie whereby someone had a vision. In the movie the vision was crystal clear, the message was crystal clear. Naturally movies are often a little different from everyday life. Some people do have visions which are very clear indeed. I used to have visions in this way and from time to time I still do. My visual experiences would come across as snap shots and

they would always be in black and white. I remember on one occasion seeing a snap shot of my friend's husband surrounded in white light. I could not quite make what the meaning of this was as the gentleman concerned was fit and healthy. A few days later I saw my friend and she looked dreadful. Her husband had died the day before.

Many people also receive visual messages in the form of shapes, symbols or even numbers. Sometimes the meaning takes a little time to interpret and at other times the meaning may quickly and easily become understood.

A few years ago, as my father lay dying, I saw a bright light all around his body and I saw a dove fly past him. A feather floated down and as I watched it, it disappeared into the air. Now, whenever I feel lost or whenever I ask for direction I often see a white feather and I know that I am being guided, watched over and on the right path. When I go to visit my father's grave I frequently see a white feather by the side of it. I take this as a message from him, his way of simply saying hello.

Do you receive messages visually?

The Little Voice
Does your intuition work best by talking to you? Do you often ask yourself questions and come up with some surprising answers. Do you often know, without

a shadow of a doubt that you are being guided by something much higher and greater than yourself?

Marjorie used to walk home each evening. Part of her walk home involved walking down a narrow alley. This was really part of a short cut. Marjorie had done this walk for over seven years and it had always been perfectly safe. She worked in and lived in good neighbourhoods. One particular evening, as Marjorie approached the alley she heard a voice in her head telling her no. NO! She should not walk this way home. Marjorie stopped walking, so loud was the voice in her head. She was reluctant to carry on and Marjorie decided to take the longer walk home, even though it was a cold and dark evening. The next morning Marjorie turned on the local news and she listened to the news headlines. The first item on the news was about a woman who had been robbed and stabbed. The woman had encountered her attacker down the same alley that Marjorie usually walked down and the attack occurred at round the same time that Marjorie would have walked down the alley. Marjorie was simply overwhelmed. She was horrified that she could have been the victim of this brutal attack and she felt sadness and empathy for the woman who had been hurt. Marjorie vowed to NEVER again ignore the little voice in her head. As a consequence of this, Marjorie has now changed jobs and moved home. She feels as if she is being guided by her little voice and she knows that her life has taken a turn for the better.

Have you an inner voice, one of intuition, which offers guidance at times in need? If this is the way that your intuition guides you then perhaps you can use this skill to help you become more creative in your work, or hobbies, or even make sound financial decisions.

Kinetic Energy: Do You Feel the Vibrations?

Do you make decisions based on how you feel? I know that we all do from time to time. Perhaps you have gone to the movies because you have felt like it, or not gone to a party because you did not feel up to it. What I am talking about here is more than that. Some people have a wonderful inner sense, a connection to energy and vibrations which often enables them to make the right decision for them at a particular time.

Have you ever:

Walked into a room and sensed an atmosphere: Either good or bad?

- Had a feeling that a particular person is going to phone you and shortly afterwards they do. Perhaps this happens so often that you have given up saying that you were just thinking about them because it has begun to sound odd!

- Have you ever sensed that you or someone close to you was ill and this has turned out to be true even before a visit to the doctor?

- Have you ever felt drawn to a particular person and then found out that they share the same interests or hobbies?

Energy is all around us. Some people believe that objects carry energy and vibrations. Some have psychic experiences when holding jewellery or items of clothing which someone else has worn.

As a Reiki Master I hold a particular interest in the human energy field. When working with clients I begin a Reiki treatment by scanning the body. This involves running my hands parallel an inch or so over the body as I feel for areas of hot or cold. Any changes within the energy field indicate that there is an energy imbalance and the imbalance is often an indication of potential illness or of disease.

The Reiki treatment is used to help the client on many levels: mentally spiritually and emotionally. The Reiki energy helps to repair the auric field. The aura consists of several layers. Damage to any of the layers is like having a hole in a curtain. Over time this spreads until the whole curtain (body) is damaged. People who pay attention to their bodies often know themselves that something is wrong. Quite often a person may seek a medical opinion only to be informed that there is nothing wrong with them. The doctor may even be annoyed with them for wasting time! Still the person continues to feel unwell but just does not know why.

All of our interactions involve energy. Everything we do, all of our activities involve the exchange of energy.

Imagine this: You see a friend and engage in conversation with them. Your friend is talking about an upcoming trip. She is really excited and tells you about all of the things that she intends to see and do on her trip. After the conversation has ended you both go your separate ways and, as you carry on with your business, think about how you feel? You are most likely to feel happy. Perhaps you feel a little envious; you might wish that you were going on this trip as well. You may feel this way especially if money is tight or you have not been on a vacation for a while. Generally it is reasonable to say that you are feeling good inside. This is because you have exchanged positive energy with another person. Positive energy, thoughts and activities are of a high vibrational frequency and lead to feelings of well-being.

Now, imagine that instead of having an enjoyable and happy conversation with your friend you had the opposite. Your friend is angry. This anger was mainly directed at her boss for giving someone else a promotion instead of her. Your friend knows that she was better at her job and that she had more experience than this other person but still she got overlooked. As you part ways after the conversation has ended you find that you feel tired and low. This is because your friend has lots of negative energy and this has been transferred to you.

Negative energy is of a low vibrational frequency and it seems to sap the life force out of a person, animal or even a plant.

If you are sensitive to the energy you will know what people, situations and events to avoid if possible.

This is Hannah's Story:

Hannah is thirty five years old. She works as a receptionist in a doctor's surgery. Hannah used to like her job, she liked the contact with people and she liked the use of medical terminology and the contact with other departments and medical services. Due to staff cutbacks some of Hannah's colleagues were made redundant and this resulted in more work for Hannah and the remaining staff. At first all the extra work seemed like a challenge for Hannah. The days went quickly, all seemed to be going well. Then a colleague went off sick and Hannah found that she was really struggling to cope. She began to develop a sore throat and her voice went a little croaky. Hannah found that she was not so quick and effective at dealing with the patients and some of them got quite angry at times. Hannah also found that she began to feel tired all of the time. The endless paperwork and the long hours began to become quite tiresome. Even activities which she normally enjoyed became a burden to her. She stopped seeing her friend Emma on Wednesday evenings and she stopped going to her keep fit classes as well. She simply did not have the energy.

During her two week vacation Hannah went to visit her sister, Michelle. During the two weeks away from work Hannah found that she began to feel like her old self. She began to laugh and joke and she even stopped having the aches and pains in her joints that had also begun to plague her life. Hannah had begun to feel old. At the age of thirty five she knew that this was wrong. Spending time with Michelle gave Hannah a new zest for life. She began to feel like her usual self. She found that she was laughing and joking with her nieces and she woke each morning looking forward to the day ahead.

Feeling more like herself she began to reassess her life. As part of her personal evaluation Hannah came to see me for a Reiki session. I noticed that there were some energy blockages around the throat area and around the heart. Hannah told me that when she was at work she had experienced a persistent sore throat. I had discovered that the Throat Chakra was out of balance.

The Throat Chakra is part of the Chakra system. Energy flows through the physical body in subtle energy channels called Nadis, this is Sanskrit word meaning riverbed. There are over 72,000 Nadis in the human body. Now imagine a network of rivers flowing around the body, there are various points where these networks cross over; a Chakra is any location where 2 or more Nadis cross over. A Chakra looks like a spinning disc or wheel. When there is dis-harmony in the body the Chakra will spin either too quickly or too slowly. If the Chakra is not correctly balanced dis-ease will result. Chakras can be balanced by energy work such as Reiki, meditation whereby the individual focusing on balancing the Chakras and by releasing the emotions which have caused the imbalance in the first place. Knowing yourself and developing your intuition are important skills in maintaining optimum health.

Going back to Hannah, she knew that she enjoyed working with people. She had thought that she had wanted to work in a medical setting but she now knew that this was too stressful, the energy in the doctor's surgery was too negative for her; sapping her life force each time she engaged with another person who was feeling low themselves. The grey waiting room and the stressed out doctors as well as the over worked staff all contributed to Hannah feeling low and, if she had continued in this way, without a shadow of a doubt she would have become ill herself.

Hannah decided to look at other ways that she could work with people. Michelle worked in a travel agents and she told Hannah of an opening which included training and an educational programme for new staff. Hannah thought that this was exactly what she was looking for. With Michelle's help, Hannah got the job and she enjoys it tremendously. Hannah said that even though she has some work pressure from time to time she really enjoys working with people in a positive setting. People are generally happy when they book their vacation and she has even been on a few vacations herself! Hannah's health has improved tremendously. Gone are the aches and pains, her voice is back to normal and she is able to see her friend Emma on a Wednesday night as well as go to her keep fit classes.

Hannah has got her life back.

- Are negative energy and a negative environment affecting your life?

- Here is a check list to help you identify negativity in your life:

- How do you feel when at work and when at home? What is your body trying to tell you?

- Do you put off carrying out certain tasks because even the thought of carrying out the task makes you feel physically sick?

- Do you have aches, pains and headaches in a particular environment or when around a particular person?

Try to avoid contact with people who do not leave you feeling good about yourself. If you have to maintain contact, try to keep this to a minimum if at all possible. When around negative people use an imaginary shield for protection. Imagine that your body is covered with an invisible shield of white or gold. Any negative words or comments will just bounce off the shield thereby protecting you. This really works, try it and see for yourself. The next time you meet with someone that you know is a little energy vampire, someone who usually leaves you feeling tired and drained try putting up your invisible shield. You will be surprised at the results. Just remember to take it down when you do not need it or you may find that people who you want and expect to approach you suddenly do not do so. This is because the person has sensed that there is something wrong and keeps away. You can close down your shield by simply imaging that it has disappeared or you can choose to say something like "shield down" and it disappears. This is because you have put those words out to the universe and what you have created in your mind you can then destroy.

I have a friend who imagines that there are lions standing guard outside of her house when she is away. My friend lives in an area where properties are often broken into and she has never been burgled. On one occasion she went on a long vacation and came home to find that both her neighbours had had their houses broken into whilst they were asleep. Her neighbours could not believe that her house was safe whilst they were burgled whilst they slept!

Your Sense of Smell

Specific smells and fragrances often bring back memories of our childhood and events in our past, some good and some not so good. Some individuals have a heightened sense of smell. Read Jessica's story:

The following morning after her uncle died Jessica could smell his pipe. There was also a feeling that her uncle was in the room, but for Jessica the primary, heightened sense was at of smell. For quite a while after her uncles death Jessica could still smell her uncle's pipe. She mentioned this to her mother and a friend of the family one afternoon. Her mother's friend told her that it was not uncommon for people to see, hear and smell things that are connected to the departed. The well-meaning family friend said that this was just part of the bereavement process. As this comment was made almost a year after her uncle's death, Jessica thought that she may need therapy, thinking that she was unable to accept the loss of her uncle Giles.

Jessica came to see me for psychotherapy. I quickly established that she was not grieving. I advised Jessica to talk to her uncle Giles whenever he was in the room and it was practical and safe to do so. After our third session together Jessica said that she had to re-schedule our next appointment for two weeks away instead of the following week as she had a business trip. During the next appointment she told me that the trip had involved her going to another city. Jessica did not know her way around so she purchased a street map. Not really looking where she was stepping Jessica was just about to walk into the road when she smelt a strong and over whelming smell of pipe smoke. Jessica stopped in her tracks and narrowly avoided being hit by a delivery truck. Jessica said that she knew without a shadow of a doubt that her uncle had saved her life. She began talking to him whenever she was alone and could smell his pipe. Jessica said that she now asks her uncle for guidance whenever she has a problem and she finds that the answer comes into her head. She said that it is like having a therapist at home with her! Jessica also said that she feels some comfort in knowing that her uncle has not gone forever and she strongly believes that she will meet him again in the after-life. Jessica now medicates as she believes that the will further develop her senses and she has also developed as a person believing that she is a lot less sceptical and judgemental than she was a year or so ago.

Have you ever smelt a perfume or fragrance that you strongly associate with a departed friend or loved one?

Has this smell come to you at a time of need, perhaps when you have been in need of advice or when you have been depressed or sad?

Have you ever smelt a fragrance and then seen or heard the person who it is connected to?

Clairgustance: What Can You Taste?

Clairgustance means clear tasting. This is the least common way to develop your intuition but some individuals have this ability which can clearly work well on its own.

Have you ever had a taste in your mouth that you can clearly associate with another person?

Perhaps you can taste granny's cookies just before she calls you?

Having the intuitive ability of taste can offer you a warning to stay away from dangerous people or places when you experience a bad taste or an unpleasant sensation in your mouth. The opposite can also be true with you experiencing pleasant sensations and tastes reminding you of pleasant experiences.

Clairgustance can be used in everyday life and at work. If you have the ability to develop this particular sense you may use it to assist decision making at work and in your home life. Medical intuitives have the ability to taste blood or experience the taste of a particular medical condition that a person died from. Nutritional practitioners can taste a particular food in connection to their patients and therefore they can identify the nutrient that is missing from the diet. For example the taste of an orange indicates a vitamin C deficiency.

By now you will have discovered which of your senses is the most developed. You may also have a secondary sense which is nearly as highly developed as the first. In the next section you will discover exercises which will help you begin to develop your senses further. Try the exercises and see for yourself.

PRACTICAL EXERCISES TO DEVELOP YOUR INTUITION

I believe in intuition and inspiration. I sometimes feel that I am right. I do not know that I am.
Albert Einstein

Before You Start
Unless instructed otherwise, before you begin any of these exercises please ensure that you have found a quiet place where you will not be disturbed.

Carry out this simple breathing exercise: Sit quietly on a chair in a comfortable position. Keep your back straight but not rigid, you need to be comfortable! Take a deep breath in through your nose for a count of 4. Hold for a count of 2. Then breathe out through your mouth for a count of 4. Keep breathing in this way for 3 to 5 minutes. This exercise is important because it enables you to close down all of the external distractions and focus internally. You will find that you are more easily able to focus on any changes and subtle messages that your senses are telling you.

Remember to turn off your phone and remove any electronic equipment from the room as you will not want the low vibrational frequency to interfere with any potential experiences you may have.

Keep a journal or diary as this may help you to remember your experiences. You will also be able to keep track of how you have progressed later.

Finally, ensure that you are not hungry, thirsty or have a need for the bathroom. You will not be able to relax and concentrate if you have a need for any of the above!

Automatic Writing
Below are 2 good exercises for you to loosen up as you begin to develop your intuition. Before you start, read all of the information below at least once so that you know what you are doing.

Begin by carrying out the breathing exercise noted above. Ensure that you also have a note book and a good pen.

Exercise One
Keep your hand relaxed and begin by placing the pen on the paper. Remember to relax your hand as some people go rigid at this point!

Now begin writing.

Write down whatever words come into your head. The words do not have to make sense. Do not try and analyse them. Keep writing for as long as your hand keeps moving. When you first try this exercise you may be writing for a few minutes, you may even work up at an hour!

When you have stopped take a deep breath in through your nose and out through your mouth.

Now, take a good look at what you have written.

You may be surprised as this may not even look like your writing. Have a look through the words on the paper, you may find patterns or even whole sentences. The words that you recognise, write them out neatly at the bottom of the page. By writing the words out again in this way you have the opportunity to think about the words that you are writing and their relevance to you. You will also be able to easily refer back to what is written instead of trying to decipher what could later appear to be jumbled up writing.

Automatic Writing: Asking a Specific Question
This exercise is great if you are trying to solve a problem, or would like an answer to a specific question.

Begin by carrying out the breathing exercise noted above. Remember to take time to slow down your thoughts and your mind from external distractions.

Have your notepad ready and relax your hand.

Read through all of the information below before you start.

Now begin by asking a specific question such as:

- How can I find a better job?

- When will I find my soul mate?

Only ask one question per session otherwise you will be confused by the answers!

Now relax your mind and write down the words that come to you.

When writing during this exercise you will find that the writing is a little slower. This is because you are been given answers to a specific question.

You will know that the exercise has ended when you have stopped writing and you will also have a feeling that it is now time to stop.

Now have a look at what you have written.

Can you find the answer to the question that you asked?

If you can, then once again make a note at the bottom of the page for clarity.

You can carry out this exercise daily if you are looking for a solution to a problem. There is no right or wrong here. Allow your intuition to guide you. Don't worry if you do not find the answer to your question during the first session, the answer will come; it just takes a little patience and practice.

Please note that there may be times when you may become frightened or distressed by what you have written. Do not be alarmed. This is simply your subconscious mind allowing its thoughts to come through to the surface.

Developing Your Visual Perception

There are 2 ways to develop your sense of visual perception. You may choose to work on yourself, or to work on other people, or you might want to try a little of both. Read all of the information below first before deciding what you would like to do.

Working on Yourself

Begin by finding a quiet place and by carrying out the breathing exercises as noted at the beginning of this section.

Exercise One – Finding an Answer to Your Problems by Visualising

- Close your eyes.

- Ask yourself a question.

- Now focus on what you can see.

When you start carrying out this exercise you may find that your mind wanders and it appears hard to establish any kind of answer. The secret is to allow your visualisations to simply drift by, allow them to drift along like clouds. When you have finished note down what you saw. You will know when the exercise has ended when you have stopped receiving visual images.

This exercise can be carried out for a few minutes or up to an hour at a time. The latter is suitable to an individual who is experienced in carrying out this exercise or to someone who is used to meditating.

Exercise Two - Out Of Body Visualisation

Many of us have heard of stories whereby a person reports an out of body experience. These are often similar to near-death experiences. If you have ever had any of these experiences I am sure you know that there is nothing to be afraid of. You can develop your ability to visualise in this way. Your physical and astral bodies are meant for travel.

- Begin with the usual exercises as noted above.

- Now close your eyes.

- Allow all thoughts to pass as if they are travelling on gentle white clouds.

- Now, when your mind is quiet and still, imagine, visually, a carbon copy of yourself standing up in front of you.

- You are that body.

- Now allow yourself to lift up and travel to wherever

you decide to go

- Your mind is connected to the astral body. See all there is to see as your body travels up and away.

When you are ready, your physical body and your astral body will connect once more. You will know when this happens as you may experience a sudden jolt as the two quickly become one once again. You may also feel a little light headed and out of sorts. This is perfectly normal and in a few short moments you will feel fine.

By allowing your astral body to explore in this way you may receive answers to any questions that you have had in the past or the present. These answers will be given to you visually. Time is not static and linear and you may even have seen something in your future that you liked. If it is something that you disliked then you have the ability and insight to know that you can change this before it happens.

You may also like to try this exercise before you go to bed. Once it is time for bed simply say to yourself, before going to sleep, that you would like to an out of body experience and see what happens. You may have to make this request a few times before it works or it may work the first time for you. If you wake up during the night then note any experiences you have had. If you sleep through the whole experience you will still have some memory of what has happened during the night but it may be a little vague and blurry.

Working on Other People
When working on other people you can practice on people that you know and even on people that you do not know.

People That You Know. When around people that you know try to go beyond what is being said and what actions are being carried out. This is more than observing body language. Try to note any visualisations that come into your mind about a person. Try to look into their heart and you may be surprised at what you find. Write down a description of the mental image. Later you can look back on what you have noted down and this will allow you to establish how accurate you have been. Please note that there is no time scale to this as what you see could be something that is going to take place tomorrow or something that may happen in the distant future.

People that you do not know. This is a fun exercise to carry out when on a train, in a waiting room or whilst out and about having a coffee and sitting on your own.

Choose a person that you feel drawn to.

Do not stare at them but gently observe them and make a note of any visualisations that you are currently experiencing.

This exercise is good for practicing your visualisation skills but you will never know that what you have experienced is true or accurate because very shortly the person who you have been watching will go about their business.

Try to carry around a note book whenever possible as there are times when they may experience sudden flashes of imagines, some clear and others less so. At times the meaning of these messages will be obvious and at other times less apparent. If the message does not hold any obvious meaning do not dismiss it, the meaning may materialise later.

Exercises to Develop the "Little Voice"
If you have discovered that your intuition works best by listening to the "Little Voice" you may also be aware that this is potentially the most difficult sense to cultivate. This is because when we hear things we automatically try and strain to listen. It is as if someone has just whispered and we are trying to strain to hear what is being said. When we do this we lose the connection to our intuitive senses as we are making a conscious decision to try to listen to the message that we are receiving.

There are times, no doubt, when those who do receive messages in this way perceive themselves as crazy as hearing voices is more often than not connected with mental illness. I had a client once who came to see me for therapy after visiting a "traditional" therapist. When the client informed the therapist that he felt that someone was whispering to him in his ear, the therapist wanted to send him for a whole batch of tests which may have eventually led him to be diagnosed with a specific mental illness and being prescribed medication. When the client learnt not to be afraid he simply discovered that it was his intuition that was guiding him.

Exercise One

- Prepare as you would for any of the previous exercises.

- Imagine a ball of white light is all around your body.

- Ask out loud if there are any messages for you.

Sometimes the messages will come through as muffled sounds. You may also receive messages that sound very distant and far away or perhaps your messages will come through as if you are listening to the radio. If the messages are unclear then the next time you carry out this exercise ask that any messages are communicated clearly to you.

Exercise Two

- Just before bedtime sit at the side of the bed for a few minutes.

- Carry out the breathing exercise to centre and focus.

- Allow your mind to go blank.

- Imagine that you are wearing an earpiece and you have fine- tuned the frequency so that you can hear your messages very clearly.

- Now ask to receive any messages that are waiting for you.

At night we are often more receptive to the messages that are being sent to us via all of the senses. Our bodies become more relaxed and we are more receptive to our intuitive messages.

Exercise to Develop How You Feel

If your intuition communicates with you by your feelings, the following exercises are designed to help you to develop this ability further. There is an exercise designed so that you can work on understanding yourself and what your body and mind are trying to tell you, and three exercises which show you how to read other people. As with all of the other exercises find a quiet place where you will not be disturbed and carry out the breathing exercise to slow your mind down and focus internally. Read the exercises through at least once so that you know what is required.

Working On Yourself – How Do You Feel?

- Close your eyes and imagine that you are sitting in a bubble of white light.

- You are being comforted, nurtured and protected by the light.

- Now focus on your heart.

- What is it trying to tell you? Are you feeling sad, happy or just okay? Is your heart telling you to make some changes in your life? Your heart tells you what is good for your soul and will help you understand your life purpose.

- When you feel as if there are no further messages from the heart turn your focus to your body. Do you have any aches or pains? Do you have any tightness around the throat which indicates that you need to say or communicate something to another person? Perhaps your back and shoulders are stiff? This could be because you are taking on too much or you are around a person who causes you to feel uptight and you hold much inside of yourself, too rigid to let go. Whatever you feel make a note in your mind.

- When you are ready to finish the session close your eyes. Take a deep breath in through your nose and end the session by gently breathing out through your mouth and opening your eyes.

Now I want you to make as many notes as you can about the session. What messages did you have from your heart and from your body? If you find this too difficult to manage in one session you could carry out this exercise by focusing on the heart in one session and later by focusing on your mind in another. Use your intuition to guide you at all times. Go with what feels best for you and what you feel that you need.

Working on Other People

When you are around other people what messages do you receive? One of the signs that someone is highly intuitive is that they feel as if their senses are overwhelmed when in crowds, at parties and on packed buses and trains – just about everywhere where there are lots of people. Why is this? Well, this is because their senses are receiving so many messages that it is causing confusion. It is like watching twenty television sets all at the same time and, even though you would not be consciously aware of it, your subconscious mind is taking it all in and your intuition is processing it as well, all at the same time. The individual feels so much pressure they feel as if they are going to burst!

So that you do not become overwhelmed to begin with, this exercise is best carried out with one or two people that you know. As you interact with them notice any subtle messages that you are receiving. The message may come through as a feeling and then transfer via a secondary sense. This is best explained by example: at times I have feelings that someone is lying to me. This comes to me intuitively and it is just something that I can feel. The message is then transferred either visually - so I see the word "Liar" in my mind's eye, or I hear the word gently being whispered to me. Whatever you sense, make notes in your notebook so that you can refer to them at a later date.

As a Reiki Master when I meet someone, especially for the first time, I sense that person's energy field and can pick up messages. I receive subtle messages on how a person is feeling and I become aware of any blockages in the energy field in a few short minutes. This is something that has taken me a while to become good at and, as you are reading this book as a beginner, I do not want you to become disillusioned if you are unable to pick this up the first time. I simply want you be aware of what is possible. You may even eventually be able to pick up messages such as any illnesses that a person has.

Exercise Three

Ask a friend or family member for a piece of jewellery. Try to obtain something that is frequently used as there will be a good connection to it. Close your eyes and hold the jewellery in one hand. Can you feel the vibrations? What messages are you receiving? Later, try with another friend's jewellery and note the differences.

Developing Your Sense of Smell
Exercise One

This first exercise is a little different as I want you to notice, via your sense of smell, what is all around you. For this you need to be carrying out your daily activities and, several times a day, I want you to stop what you are doing and note down what you can smell. You may choose to simply stop walking and note down what you can smell. You may try this on a bus or train or even whilst sitting at your desk at work.

The purpose of this exercise is to finely tune your sense of smell as you become increasingly more aware of scents and smells all around you. As your senses develop you will become aware of any smells which are out of place. For example, you may stop walking in the park and suddenly notice a strong smell of roses even though it is deep winter with snow on the ground. If this happens accept the experience and try to understand the message behind it. Ask yourself what the message is and pretty soon I am sure the answer will come to you. If there are times that you smell unpleasant or frightening smells do not be afraid. This is simply a message that there is something that you need to change in your life or a person or situation that you need to keep away from.

Exercise Two - Develop Your Sense of Smell

Try this exercise around other people. When interacting with others what can you smell? Naturally, there will be the smells of perfumes, aftershave and other fragrances. There could be food smells or alcohol depending on the situation. Try to go deeper. Notice any unusual smell. I know of a nurse who states that she can smell diabetes on her patients even before they have been diagnosed. With practice there is no limit on what your sense of smell can tell you. Try it, find out for yourself.

Developing Your Sense of Taste
If you are fortunate to have the intuitive ability to work with the oral sensations of taste then you are very lucky because it is the one sense that intuitively most people find difficult to develop.

Exercise One - Develop Your Natural Sense of Taste

Here is a way to fine tune your taste buds: take a small amount of your favourite food and find somewhere quiet where you will not be disturbed. Now, begin by eating one mouthful at a time. As you chew see if you can identify specific ingredients if at all possible. For example if you are eating a biscuit that contains vanilla essence see if you can taste the vanilla. You can practice this exercise as often as you like and you will become a master at identifying specific tastes, as well as finding that you become more satisfied easily at meal times as you are really chewing your food and nourishing your body.

Exercise Two

Identify when you are having an intuitive experience. Is the taste pleasant or not? What is the intuitive message that you are being sent? When you have an experience in this way note down as soon as possible exactly what you can taste and when the taste first became apparent. By noting down what you experience you will quickly and easily begin to notice that certain tastes have specific meanings for you and you will begin to more easily understand the messages that you receive.

As you carry out these exercises please try and remember to enjoy the experiences.

The more you relax and enjoy what you are doing the quicker and easier the messages will come to you.

Practice does make perfect and there will be times when you feel frustrated and feel that this is really not working out for you likewise there will be other times when you feel that you really have got to grips with working well with your intuition.

As it is impossible to isolate your senses, you may find that you receive a message via one sense and then it is quickly transferred to another. For example you may receive a visual message followed by a specific feeling. Go with what works best for you, it is your way of communicating after all.

HOW TO MEET YOUR SPIRIT GUIDE

All my thoughts, words and actions are guided

Please note that you do not necessarily have to complete this exercise in order to develop your intuition. Some people may feel uncomfortable or not yet ready to meet their spirit guide. You will know when and if you are ready. If the time is not yet right for you it is okay, you can always refer back to this section at a later stage.

Allow between 15 minutes and half an hour for this exercise.

Read the whole exercise through at least once (possibly more) so that you know what you have to do and so that you do not lose your concentration and connection to your guide at a later stage by having to read through this section again when you are meditating.

- Begin by finding a quiet place where you will not be disturbed.

- Sit in a comfortable position.

- When you are ready close your eyes.

- Breathe normally and notice the pattern of your breathing. As you focus in this way begin to feel yourself slowly relaxing further and further down.

- Imagine that you are inside a big white ball of protective light. Feel the gentle warmth of the ball.

- Now imagine that you are standing at the top of a flight of stairs.

- The steps are safe and secure and lead down to a beautiful garden.

- I want you to slowly descend the steps one at a time, stopping at each step.

- Begin now on the 10th step.

- Step down and say to yourself the number "10". Find yourself relaxing a little more.

- Go down another step, go down to step 9.

- Allow yourself to go that bit deeper down.

- Keep going in this way all the way down to the last step.

- Pause for a moment and step down into this beautiful garden. Use all of your intuitive senses to explore all that is around you. If you have allergies or sinus problems you will find that the protection of the white light will keep the allergies away from you and you can enjoy all of the beauty that is around you.

- Begin walking through the garden. Feel the sensation of the sun on your back, warming and nurturing and not too warm or too cool. Feel the grass beneath your feet as you connect to nature. Hear the gentle sound of the sea a short distance away.

- Keep walking until in your mind you are relaxed and satisfied that you have seen all that there is to see.

- Now begin to walk over to a bench which is near to a small pond.

- You sit on the bench.

- In your mind ask to meet your spirit guide.

- And now wait.

Your guide will come to you when you are ready. Do not become impatient if your guide does not come to you straight away. This may be because the guide could feel that now is not the best time to meet you.

At some point you will feel a sense of presence. You may even physically and clearly see a presence next to you on the bench. Again, use your senses and use your intuitive abilities to fully experience what is a special time for you.

Your guide is now willing to communicate with you. Ask your guide his/her name. You may hear the name clearly or it may be a little muffled. If you do not understand it is okay to ask again. Remember that your guide has been waiting a long time to meet you and there may be messages that they wish to communicate with you. Have patience and be willing to wait as your guide may simply sit with you for a while before communicating any messages. When your guide is ready you may physically see them disappear, or you may feel via any of your other senses that they have gone away now. You might even hear the words "goodbye" whispered to you as they leave.

- In your own time stand up from the bench.

- Walk through the garden and begin to ascend the steps.

- As you walk up each step feel yourself becoming more and more alert.

- When you are at the top step imagine that the bubble of light has disappeared.

- Now step up from that top step and open your eyes.

- Give yourself a few moments to adjust and become alert and back in time with your usual environment.

Now is the time to make a note of what has happened. When you first meet your guide it is often a truly amazing experience. You can carry out this meditation as many times as you wish. Some people prefer to meet with their guides for direction and to help them answer difficult questions or to solve problems. You can talk to your guide in your daily live and remember to pay attention to the clues that they leave to remind you of their presence and to direct you such a feathers and symbols that have specific meaning to you.

If you have not met your guide during your first session do not worry. Keep carrying out this exercises and your guide will come to you. Your patience will be rewarded in the end!

Very rarely you may encounter a feeling that you have attracted an undesirable entity to you. Do not be afraid. This is not your guide and all you have to do is ask them to go away. Imagine the white light like a thick bubble all around you protecting you.

Now open your eyes. You can let go of the bubble of light as it has done its job of protecting you and you can now become fully alert and aware of your environment.

INTUITIVE HEATH

My body and mind glow with health and vitality
Your mind and your body are always sending you messages. When you were a baby your body would tell you that you were hungry or tired. You would respond to those messages by crying and your caregiver would attend to your needs. Once your needs were satisfied you would stop crying until your body sent another signal to the brain for something else.

As we grow and develop we somehow condition ourselves not to pay attention to the signals that our bodies send us. When we have an ache in a joint we might say that we are getting old if we are of a certain age or if the pain is only present in certain situations we might dismiss it. How do you know when something intuitively feels right or wrong?

Think for a moment about something that feels right. You might choose to think about your vacation, a visit to the movies or meeting up for lunch with an old friend. What sort of feelings do you have? When I am thinking of something that feels right for me I can feel the vibrations in my energy field increase, I can feel my aura expand, I have a gut feeling that makes me feel good. Note down how you feel. How often do you feel like this?

Now I want you to think of something that makes you feel bad. I want you to choose a personal experience for this, so please try, even if it is a little painful. You might decide to choose when you were told off by your boss, when you had a disagreement with a loved one, or even when you turned in the opposite direction after you saw someone mugged. Again, I want you to note down how you feel. When I feel like this I feel my energy field shrink down and appear close to my body. I feel anxious and defensive inside. I may even feel like lashing out. How often do you feel like this?

Now I want you to concern yourself with how you feel most of the time. Do you feel mostly good or mostly bad feelings? This is similar to an exercise that you carried out earlier on in this book. Now that you are more intuitive, and have a greater understanding and connection with your feelings, it is important to carry out this exercise. If you feel mostly good feelings then you know that you are on the right path. If you have mostly bad feelings then you need to pay attention to what your body and your mind is trying to tell you. Begin to ask yourself when and where you feel this way. It is best to keep a journal for a week or so as this will enable you to notice any patterns which might emerge. Are the feelings connected to a particular person, a place or a job or even a chore? Your feelings are the way in which your body is trying to communicate with your mind. It is tapping gently away trying to get your attention. Do any of the following sound familiar:

- Your body feels heavy and tired when you do certain things.

- You have aches and pains for no apparent reason.

- Backache when your boss is present in the room.

- An upset stomach especially on a Monday morning before going to work, or over the weekend when you relax and let go.

- Tightness around the throat or chest.

- Feelings of dizziness.

When you were a child is it likely that if you had a tummy ache before going to school your parents would have sent you anyway. In this way we learn to ignore the signals that our body is sending us. Please do not get me wrong here as there are times when we have to do difficult and unpleasant things. What I am talking (or rather writing!) about are the things in your day to day life that you do often, or all of the time that are so far from your life's purpose that these tasks or activities are making you ill.

I have often wondered why people get old and sick. In fact when we mention the word age I am not really certain which part of our bodies we are talking about. Below are a few facts:

- The skin renews itself every 2 to 3 weeks. Many people are familiar with this concept.

- Your lungs are 6 weeks old.

- Your liver is 5 months old.

- Your heart is 20 years old. This is relatively recent discovery as it has been found that there are stem cells around the heart.

Given the above facts why do we become sick? It is my personal, intuitive view, through the experiences that I have noted as a Reiki master and practitioner and as a psychotherapist, that people become ill when there is a discrepancy between what they would like to do and what they feel that they are able to do given their circumstances. Your body lets you know when something is wrong by sending you subtle messages at first. Then the knocking on the door becomes louder if you refuse to listen.

Anxiety is also a contributing factor to the illness. A client came to see me who wished to be treated for anxiety. He told me that in the first instance the anxiety began at work when he had to give a presentation to a boss who he did not get along with. Slowly, slowly his anxiety grew until he felt that he could no longer be in the same room as his boss. At home he began to develop OCD symptoms. He had to check all of the doors in the house three times to ensure that they were locked before leaving the home. The final crunch came when he was unable to travel in the lift up to his office. Feeling the lift closing in on him and the doors appearing to sway he jumped out at the first opportunity and rushed home. Interestingly, this client was due to have an endoscopy as he was having trouble swallowing but had to cancel due to his anxiety. After a number of sessions and time off sick from work it was established that he was in the wrong profession and when he took matters into his own hands and began to make some life changes (including getting a different job) his health improved. He did have the endoscopy and everything was fine.

In the same way that we may be inclined to talk louder and louder when we engage in conversation with a deaf person, our body will keep sending out messages and signals until we really stop and listen.

If we need to stop and slow down we may know this on a conscious level but choose to ignore it believing that we have too much to do. We then develop a cold and MAY slow down. If we do we use the cold as an excuse. We then feel that we are not to blame if chores do not get done or tasks are not completed. We say, hey it's the cold. Often we are secretly pleased that this has happened. We are secretly pleased that we have been made to stop rushing around and doing things. Often we do not listen to what the message was. We ignore the intuitive messages which have told us that we feel much better now that we have stopped doing something or have slowed down. Once we are better we carry on in the same old way, how crazy is that?

So, our intuition bangs a little harder on the door and we develop another illness which is likely to be more serious and significant than the first. Along with the illness, anxiety begins to develop. We feel that something is wrong often before we become symptomatic. When we are forced to slow down again, hopefully, we take on board the message. If we do not there are dire consequences.

When I talk to people who have recovered from serious and significant illness they often tell me that there illness was really a blessing in disguise. Forced to stay at home or even in bed they have had a lot of time to reflect on their lives. In this way they become connected with their core and connect with their life's purpose. For those who are creative they may begin to once again take up the skills that they had let just drift away. The anxiety nearly always disappears as they connect with their true life path, their destiny. For some, even if they have to go back to the job that they thought caused the illness in the first place, they now look at the job with new eyes. They can see that it was not the job but the way that they viewed it that was the problem. Learning a valuable life lesson will teach you to enjoy rather than endure your life. Make time for the things that you intuitively enjoy will create a wealth of riches and open new doors for you.

Intuitive Body Awareness
Below is an exercise to help you become aware of the subtle messages that your body is trying to tell you.

Begin in your usual way by finding a quiet place and concentrating on your breathing. Remember to breathe in through your nose for a count of 4, hold for a count of 2 and breathe out through your mouth for a count of 4.

Please read through this entire exercise before you begin so that you fully understand what to do.

- Imagine that there is a small ball of light hovering over your head.

- What feelings are you are coming to the surface? Are you worried about something that you have not told someone else about? Do you need to share a secret with a friend?

- When the messages have stopped coming through allow the ball of light to travel to your throat.

- What do you feel? Do you need to communicate something to someone else no matter how unpleasant? Again note any messages that you receive.

- Now move on to the heart. What do you feel? What is your heart trying to tell you? Do you feel anxious and is your heart beating too fast as it tries to communicate with you?

- Now I want you to allow the ball of light to drift anywhere that you feel it needs to go. Be guided by your intuition. Do you feel pain in your foot or knee? Think about what the message is trying to tell you.

- When you are ready allow the ball of light to lift up and away from you.

- Further and further away from your body.

You now feel connected to your body and soul and you can now take the time to write down any messages which have been communicated via your intuition. You now have the ability and tools to act on these messages. Do so for your own health and wellbeing.

DAILY AFFIRMATIONS

You are always more than enough
As you develop your sense of intuition you will find that you will begin to spend more time focusing internally rather than externally. You will begin to become less bothered and worried about the small things around you. Being less inclined to worry and fuss over the small things you will be more focused on either discovering your life's purpose, or working at something that is meaningful to you in your life. We were not put on this earth to carry out a routine of the same thing day in day out, as we were not meant for a life of drudgery. When we set ourselves goals we may find that at times it may be difficult to maintain focus and this is where the daily affirmations come in.

It is really important to spend a few quiet minutes alone each day. Your body and mind need that time to absorb all that has happened during the day, as well as having time to heal. Once you have established time just for you, you will begin to look forward to it and you will also notice the difference when you are unable to manage this.

Now begin your session by just sitting quietly alone for a few minutes with your eyes open. Allow any thoughts about the day just drift into your mind. Do not try to analyse them.

When you are ready close your eyes and carry out the breathing exercise that I have mentioned frequently throughout this book. Naturally there are many other forms of meditation and this exercise is just a simple one for you to learn to begin to focus. You may wish to do further research and find the best style of meditation for you.

Now that you are in a naturally relaxed state I want you focus internally. Your subconscious mind and your intuition will guide you into a totally relaxed state. Below I have written some affirmations for you. I want you to begin by going with the ones which you are drawn to. Later, you can take time out and develop your own. Your subconscious mind does not know the difference between what is real and what is not. By saying your daily affirmations your mind will accept that this is reality. It is really important to say the affirmation from the heart. You must believe in what you are saying for it to work. Repeat the affirmation 3 times. Do not choose more than 3 affirmations at any one time. Here is a small list for you to choose from so that you can get started:

- I trust my intuition with a deep sense of security.

- All that I want and need comes easily and quickly.

- I am an abundant person.

- I am strong.

- I am healthy.
- I have let go of my past.
- I trust my inner wisdom.
- I am glowing with health and happiness.
- I have all the time I need.
- My mind is calm and relaxed.
- I always think clearly.
- I am focused on my goals.
- My inner vision guides me.
- I am full of energy and vitality.
- I always make good use of my time.
- My thoughts turn into reality.
- I sleep well.
- I do not allow others to deter me from my goals.
- I love to exercise.
- I look forward to meditating and spending some quality time alone.
- I feel happiness deep in my heart.

- I am drawn to positive people.
- I enjoy nourishing my body with healthy food.
- I pay attention to the messages from my senses.
- Only I know that I CAN do it.
- I do not need reassurance from others.
- I seek advice but trust my intuition.
- I always have more than enough.
- My guide will show me the way.
- I listen to what my heart is telling me.
- I heal quickly.
- I am content at this moment.

A FINAL NOTE FROM THE AUTHOR

I hope that you have enjoyed reading "A Beginners Guide to Developing Your Intuition", I have certainly enjoyed writing it. I hope that you are now inspired to seek intuitive guidance whenever possible. I know that my own life has been much more fulfilling and enjoyable since I began to listen to what my body and mind was telling me. I wish you good luck in all that you do from the bottom of my heart. Farewell my friend.

Also By Marion McGeough

If you have enjoyed reading this book about developing your intuition you may also be interested in the following:

Books

- Crystal Healing and the Human Energy Field: A Beginners Guide.

- A Beginner's Guide to the Chakras.

- Shoden: The definitive guide to first degree Reiki: Mindfulness, Meditation, Reiki treatments and more.

- A Beginner's Guide to Mindfulness.

Hypnosis CD
- Overcome Your Fear of Flying.

All products are available from Amazon.

If you wish to contact Marion here are her details.

Website: www.britishacademyofreiki.co.uk
Email address: marionreiki@yahoo.co.uk

Printed in Great Britain
by Amazon